The Alma Mater of a Nation

THE COLLEGE OF

WILLIAM AND MARY

1693

PHOTOGRAPHY BY DAN DRY

INTRODUCTION BY WILFORD KALE

HARMONY HOUSE

PUBLISHERS LOUISVILLE

Executive Editors : William Butler and William Strode
Director of Photography : William Strode
Library of Congress Catalog Number 86-082734
Hardcover International Standard Book Number 0-916509-12-5
Printed in USA by Pinaire Lithographing Corp., Louisville, Kentucky
First Edition printed March, 1987, by Harmony House Publishers
P.O. Box 90, Prospect, Kentucky 40059 (502) 228-2010 / 228-4446
Copyright © 1987 by Harmony House Publishers
Photographs copyright © Dan Dry

We are grateful to many people at the College who participated
in the research, production or review phases of this book. From the
Society of the Alumni they are : Scott Cunningham, Executive Vice-
President of the Society of the Alumni ; Merchandising Director
Victor Orozco ; and Alumni Information Officer Frankie Martens.
From the College are : Public Information Director Elaine Justice ;
Director of Publications S. Dean Olson ; Archivists Laura Parrish
and Carter Harris ; and student liaison J.D. Bowers. Special thanks
also to Wilford Kale, whose book *Hark Upon The Gale* was the
primary source material for the history section of this book.

INTRODUCTION

By Wilford Kale, '66

"Its classic halls are closed and deserted. From a once flourishing faculty, which early and ably represented both history and political science with other liberal arts, only the president… now remains.

"At the opening of every academic year, in October [Col.] Ewell causes the … bell to be rung, reminding Williamsburg that the ancient college still lives."

N.H.R. Dawson
U.S. Commissioner of Education
March, 1887

One hundred years ago, the College of William and Mary in Virginia was struggling through a period history would call "The Silent Years." The Board of Visitors still governed the school; the indomitable old president Col. Benjamin Stoddard Ewell was still in place; and faculty was appointed intermittently. But there were no students.

The College lingered from 1882 until 1888 on the brink of ruination. Ultimately, this would be the last in a series of bleak events during the 19th century which nearly led to the College's demise. In fact, three or four times, William and Mary, by all rights, should have ceased to exist as an institution of higher education.

Nevertheless, it struggled; it persevered; and it overcame. Today, it survives like the Phoenix of classical mythology, having risen from the ashes of disaster, to soar in the skies of triumph and success.

That is the spirit that is William and Mary.

One need only walk through the campus these days on a balmy afternoon to feel not only the spirit of yesterday, but also the idealism and youthful exuberance of today's students as they labor in the fields of academia, cultivating and nurturing the seeds of learning and developing the intellect that will enable them to enhance the William and Mary of tomorrow.

As one moves across the old College yard, through the main campus to the "new campus of good arts and sciences," it is easy to glimpse the full fabric of William and Mary's history, the threads of faculty, students, administration and alumni that have come together for nearly three centuries to "knit the generations each to each."

The majestic Sir Christopher Wren Building, in the heart of the colonial campus, is the oldest academic building still in use in the United States. For at least 150 years of William and Mary history it was "The College."

Begun just two years after the royal charter was granted on February 8, 1693 by King William III and Queen Mary II of England, the Wren, like the College itself, has survived fires and wars. Through the vision of Dr. J.A.C. Chandler and with the funds of philanthropist John D. Rockefeller, Jr., the Wren was restored in 1928-1931 as a pilot effort, which led later to the restoration of the city's 18th century historic area.

It is difficult to visit the building, climb the steps or walk the halls without realizing the important role this landmark played, not only in Virginia history, but also in the history of higher education in America.

The Great Hall of the Wren Building, the dining room in colonial times, frequently serves the same role today as friends of the College and alumni dine in a candlelight setting that harkens to the days when William and Mary was called the "school of statesmen."

Across the courtyard in another wing of the Wren is the chapel. Built somewhat later than the rest of the building, the chapel

Lord Botetourt

remains important in the lives of many alumni as the setting for countless weddings, baptisms and confirmations.

Flanking the Wren, also on the 18th century campus, are the President's House and the Brafferton. All William and Mary presidents have used the house as their official residence since it was built in 1732. The Brafferton, originally built in 1723 as the Indian School, today houses the offices of the president and the provost.

Throughout the 18th and much of the 19th centuries, these three buildings were the campus. But in the 20th century, major construction was undertaken and gradually, the Wren, the Brafferton and the President's House became the heart of the old campus.

For many William and Mary alumni, the new campus was the group of buildings constructed around the Sunken Garden. The neo-Georgian classroom buildings and dormitories, built in the 1920s and 1930s, housed the students and faculty who were part of a major plan to bring increased academic credibility to the College.

For thousands of other alumni, the new campus comprises the buildings built in the 1960s and 1970s in the pine woods behind the main campus. The architecture changed, but the new campus had space — space to eliminate basement laboratories, crowded lecture halls and four-professor offices. It brought a new library with shelves for all the books, bright, clean study areas and a home for Lord Botetourt.

But William and Mary is more than just bricks and mortar. It is more than the giant elms that once guarded the front campus, or Squirrel Cabin or the wonderful trails around Lake Matoaka, or the quonset huts or Crim Dell.

William and Mary is a unique spot where students fortunate enough to gain admission can find an enriching educational experience and can forge friendships to last a lifetime.

Dr. Edward E. Brickell, former College rector, in a Homecoming oration in October, 1979, probably best summed up the feelings of many alumni for this old school:

"I would hope that this institution and all in it, will always accept the challenge of trying valiantly, of daring greatly, so that the charge

given us by those early leaders will be carried out fully, to the everlasting glory of this old College and all who love it.

"...We must never lose the sense of proportion, the perspective that enables us to view events over the long reach of history, confident that come what may, this old College will endure..."

And endure it has.

The first edition of the Colonial Echo in 1899 placed the historical importance of the College in perspective; it could have been written yesterday:

"While it seems that the day of exulting in the deeds of ancestors and predecessors has passed away in this practical age of ours, and we are more concerned in grasping the problems of the living present, yet it is more than a mere fancy that the student will gain some inspiration by enrolling his name with those of our nation's greatest heroes...

"The many historical associations which cluster around William and Mary make it peculiarly appropriate as a seat of learning."

Today, we find William and Mary at the forefront of higher education nationwide. Its academic programs are ranked with America's best; it is proudly referred to as one of the "Public Ivys" — those state-supported institutions which have developed academic prowess to rival the Ivy League colleges and universities. Its students come from across the nation and the world with broad and diverse backgrounds; they bring a rich heritage of social involvement, personal concern and a desire to play major roles in the life around them.

There is something about William and Mary that has encouraged philosophical thought and scholarly investigation. From the days of a youthful Thomas Jefferson in the early 1760s and the founding of Phi Beta Kappa in 1776 to the 1980s, students at the College have maintained diligence in academic pursuits and a vigilance toward the scholarly insight that encourages the development of the educated man and woman.

There also is something about William and Mary that sets this college apart from others. While the emphasis on education is strong, there is a keen and abiding awareness that the well-rounded, creative student, who can provide leadership in campus organizations or can participate successfully on the athletic fields, is just as important.

Playing a vital role in the story that is William and Mary are the professors and teachers of the faculty, past and present. Throughout the nearly 300 years of classes, there have been important professors who have altered and shaped the course of instruction at the College with their scholarship and intellect.

Jefferson, in his writings, noted that William Small, professor of natural philosophy, "fixed the destinies of my life." Other important early faculty members included Charles Bellini, the first professor of modern languages, George Wythe, who held the first chair of law, James McClurg, first professor of medicine, and Robert Andrews, the first professor to include the fine arts in his courses. Later notables included William Barton Rogers, Nathaniel Beverley Tucker and John Millington.

At the end of the silent years, it was the famed "seven wise men" — the entire faculty — who led William and Mary into the modern era. Their names are well known: Lyon G. Tyler, J. Lesslie Hall, Thomas Jefferson Stubbs, Lyman B. Wharton, Van F. Garrett, Hugh S. Bird and Charles Edward Bishop.

Perhaps, most of all, William and Mary is students — classmates, laboratory partners, roommates, lovers, teammates, sweethearts and friends. Especially friends. People we never forget.

This is a book by which to remember William and Mary. It is not a history to list fact after fact. It is a memory book, a delightful encounter, through photography, with images that bring quickly to mind the spirit of this college.

Remember.

Barksdale Field in the early morning with dew still on the ground. Music coming from a big party along fraternity row. Spring Finals and the big dance in the Sunken Garden. Sorority rush and the Saturday morning dash across Richmond Road. The Royalist. The statue of Lord Botetourt in front of the Wren Building and Old Spotswood, the cannon, standing guard nearby.

Housemothers. Curfews, signing out, scrambling to get back before the doors were locked. Trinkle Hall. The swimming pool in Jefferson. The Deanery. Old Citizenship. The empty field before there was a Sunken Garden.

The William and Mary Choir. Old Phi Beta Kappa Hall and the marvelous William and Mary Theatre. Pep rallies. Graduation in the Wren yard. Running through the rain to your next class. Senior Day and the tolling of the bell. Long walks through the historic area. Love in bloom. The Colonial Echo. Paddling a canoe on Lake Matoaka. The handball courts.

Fog hanging heavy on the front campus. The Green Machines. Trying to find a vacant lane to swim in. Almost missing an exam. All-nighters trying to finish the term paper. Weekends with nothing to do. Football games when we won. The 25th reunion you were glad you attended. President Bryan's Christmas parties. Your old roommate.

Washington 200 and the history class. Your first campus sweetheart. The Yule Log ceremony. The Homecoming Parade and the float that won. The Flat Hat. Sororities. Fraternities. T-R-I-B-E.

Memories. That is what this book is all about. As you examine the photographs of contemporary William and Mary, let your mind wander to your own days on campus. Many things have changed, you will see. But many scenes are still the same.

Years change, but William and Mary remains. Enjoy this glimpse of the old College. Enjoy the present and enjoy the nostalgia it stimulates.

For most of us, this is more than just a college; it is a family of strong and abiding friends.

This is more than just a college; it is a home where heritage is cherished and traditions are nurtured.

This is more than just a college; it is a welcome retreat where on days like Homecoming, spirit, enthusiasm and faith can be rekindled.

This is more than just a college; it is a companion through life, a companion who never falters, a companion of which to be proud.

This is William and Mary, the college you and I love.

1691 Rev. James Blair is issued instructions by the General Assembly to found a college.

1693 King William III and Queen Mary II grant a charter to establish the College of William and Mary in Virginia; Rev. James Blair is named president; a tract of 330 acres is purchased for 170 Lbs.

1695 Constructionbegins on the Main Building, later named the Wren Building.

1700 The College Building becomes the headquarters of colonial government.

1723 The Brafferton Building erected.

1749 George Washington receives surveyors license from the College.

1750 The F.H.C. society is formed.

1756 The first honorary degree of Master of Arts from the College is conferred upon Benjamin Franklin.

1760 Thomas Jefferson attends the College, and stays to study law with George Wythe in Williamsburg.

1774 James Monroe, later the fifth president of the U.S., attends the College.

1775 A number of students and faculty join Williamsburg militia companies; classes are maintained throughout this period.

1776 Phi Beta Kappa, the first American intercollegiate Greek letter fraternity, is founded.

1779 Under the leadership of Gov. Thomas Jefferson, William and Mary becomes a university. The first American chairs of law and modern languages are established.

1781 College classes are suspended when the British army invades Virginia; they resume in the Fall of 1782.

1788 George Washington accepts office as the first American Chancellor of the College.

1801 The marble statue of Baron de Botetourt is purchased and moved to the College yard.

1859 John Tyler, 10th President of the U.S. and a student at the College in 1806, becomes Chancellor, serving until his death in 1862.

1861 President Benjamin Ewell, the professors and nearly all the students enter the Confederate army; the College Building is first used as a barracks and later as a hospital.

1865 The war ends in April, and in the Fall the College is re-opened.

1882 The College is forced to close for lack of funds. Yet the College bell is rung by President Ewell at the opening of each academic year, "reminding Williamsburg that the ancient College still lives."

1888 The College is revived under President Lyon G. Tyler, son of U.S. President John Tyler.

1893 The College fields its first football team against Norfolk Y.M.C.A., losing 16 to 0.

1906 By an act of the General Assembly all College property is transferred to the Commonwealth of Virginia.

1911 The first issue of the student newspaper, The Flat Hat, appears.

1918 By an act of the General Assembly, William and Mary becomes the first coeducational State college in Virginia.

1925 The Richmond Professional Institute becomes a division of the College.

1930 The Norfolk Division of the College is opened.

1935 Marshall-Wythe Hall, an office and classroom building, is opened.

A CHRONOLOGY OF THE COLLEGE

1935 (cont.) Marshall-Wythe Hall is subsequently named James Blair Hall; Cary Field opens as the athletic stadium.

1957 Phi Beta Kappa Memorial Hall is opened, the first building on the new campus.

1961 Dr. Paschall is inaugurated as president of the College; the Queen's Guard, a drill unit in honor of three royal benefactors of the College — Queen Mary II, Queen Anne and Queen Elizabeth II, is invested.

1964 The College of William and Mary is authorized to grant its first earned doctorate degrees — the Ph.D. in Physics and in Marine Science; the College establishes its first Graduate Council.

1965 The Virginia Associated Research Center at Newport News for the operation of NASA's Space Radiation Effects Laboratory is established.

1966 The Earl Gregg Swem Library is opened as the keystone of the modern campus of arts and sciences; the School of Education at the College of William and Mary is reestablished.

1967 William and Mary achieves university status in the modern sense. The College Board of Visitors specifies that the historic name of the "College" would remain unchanged.

1968 The School of Business Administration is established; the College Board of Visitors authorizes Christopher Newport College in Newport News, a branch of William and Mary, to become a full four-year, degree-granting college by June, 1971.

1969 William and Mary establishes its Sports Hall of Fame, inducting 34 men.

1971 Construction is completed on William and Mary Hall; Thomas Ashley Graves, Jr., associate dean in the Harvard Graduate School of Business, takes office as the 24th president of William and Mary.

1973 In an agreement between the College of William and Mary and the Society of the Alumni, Inc., the College takes over responsibility for fund-raising previously conducted by the Society, and guarantees an annual budget for the Society.

1976 The Presidential Debate, third of the 1976 campaign, between President Gerald R. Ford and Democratic nominee Jimmy Carter, is held in Phi Beta Kappa Hall.

1979 The Virginia Institute of Marine Science at Gloucester is finally integrated into the College of William and Mary.

1980 The Marshall-Wythe School of Law moves into its new multi-million dollar facility adjacent to the National Center for State Courts.

1981 HRH the Prince of Wales visits William and Mary to receive an honorary fellowship from the College; the women's golf team wins the AIAW Division II national championship, the first national title in women's sports.

1983 William and Mary dedicates the first phase of the Joseph l. and Margaret Muscarelle Museum of Art; fire partially destroys Jefferson Hall.

1984 Paul R. Verkuil, class of 1961, is named the 25th president of the College of William and Mary. Dr. Verkuil served as dean of the School of Law at Tulane; Anne Dobie Peebles is named rector of the College, the first woman so appointed in the College's 291-year history.

1987 Warren Burger, former Chief Justice of the U.S., is named the 20th Chancellor.

OF WILLIAM AND MARY

The student, male or female, must be hard-boiled indeed who does not imbibe the spirit of the atmosphere and be stimulated to higher aims. He who trods the paths once trod by our great alumni, the silent majority who even now may be peopling this hall, and feels no inspiration is dull indeed ... This College has always had a reputation for something more than scholarship. It has always been its ambition to turn out gentlemen as well as scholars.

Robert M. Hughes, Baccalaureate Address, 1933

I am enormously proud to be associated now with this famous college and to continue the family association, which began with Queen Mary's enthusiastic support all those years ago and which has survived to the present day...

HRH Prince Charles, Convocation in Phi Beta Kappa Hall,
May 2, 1981

The Sunken Garden

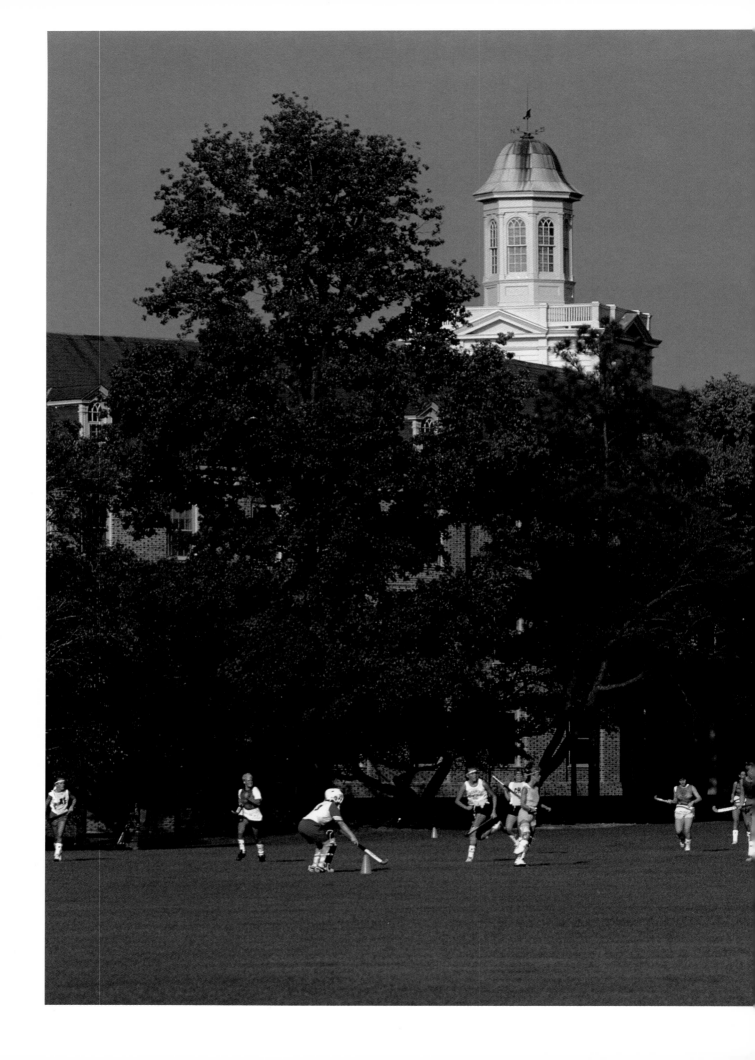

Despite the demands of changing times and circumstances, the basic mission of this College in its 268 years has remained constant: to give this Commonwealth, this Nation and the world the educated man.

Davis Y. Paschall, presidential inaugural address, 1961

Original classroom, Wren Building

Muscarelle Art Museum

36

Andrews Hall

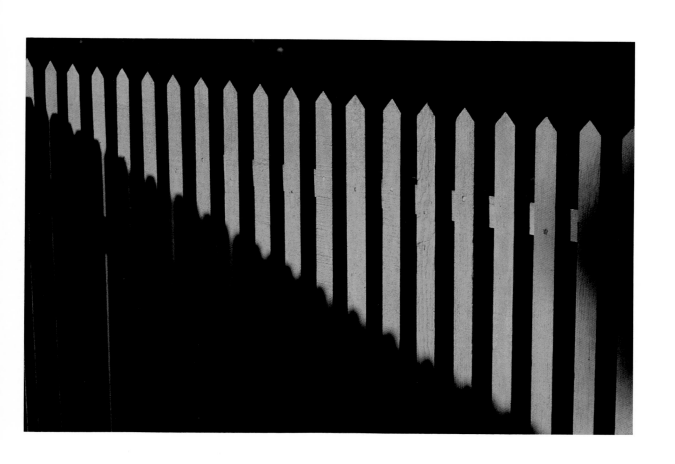

Great Hall - Wren Building

We have at this University a tradition and a foundation of teaching and learning that transcends momentary trends and swings in the pendulum of the economy. The fundamentals of liberal education, as taught here over the centuries, offers a basis of wisdom, of values, and of skills, as functional now as they will be in the lambent glow of the CRT computer screens. While we have great respect for the capabilities and potential of technology, and indeed offer many excellent courses and programs…to prepare our students for useful and productive lives in the technological society, we must not forget that at the heart lies man, the real soul of the new machines.

Thomas A. Graves, Jr., President, The College of William and Mary, Charter Day, 1983

Marshall Wythe School of Law

Rare Book Room, Earl Gregg Swem Library

When people think of higher education in Virginia, they think of William and Mary. Out of this rich quarry not mere stones have been hewed, but the makers and builders of this nation were educated in these very surroundings...

Alvin Duke Chandler, address to incoming freshmen, 1959

Queen's Guard

I cherish this link between the Crown and your College, because it is a part of our joint histories … It also demonstrates the very close association which has always existed between learning, the arts and sciences of our countries … It might surprise some of them, but I can say quite sincerely that I am very proud of the fact that this College educated so many founders of this nation. Rarely has any country been able to produce a group of such enlightened and skilled statesmen as those who gathered around George Washington.

Queen Elizabeth II, October 16, 1957

Duke of Gloucester Street, Williamsburg

The Colonial Capitol, Williamsburg

The seat of literature at Williamsburg has ever, in my view, been an object of veneration, as an institution for its communication of useful learning, and conducive to the true principles of national liberty. You may be assured that it shall receive every encouragement and benefaction in my power toward its reestablishment.

George Washington, 1781

I know of no place in the world, while the present professors remain, where I would as soon place a son.

Thomas Jefferson, 1788

So let our college stand forever as a lasting symbol of patriotic service, of unshaken faith, of magnificent history which binds the glories of the past with the hopes of the future…Hark upon the gale of history, my friends, and listen to its call.

Dr. Lyon Tyler

Interior, President's residence

One reason the alumni of this college have furnished leadership out of proportion to their numbers is that in years spent here students absorb some of the spirit manifest in her historic past. We really serve the future when we recall the past — not to live it, but to draft its inspiration.

Joseph F. Hall, Alumni Day speech, 1938

The President's Residence

Overleaf: Yule Log Ceremony

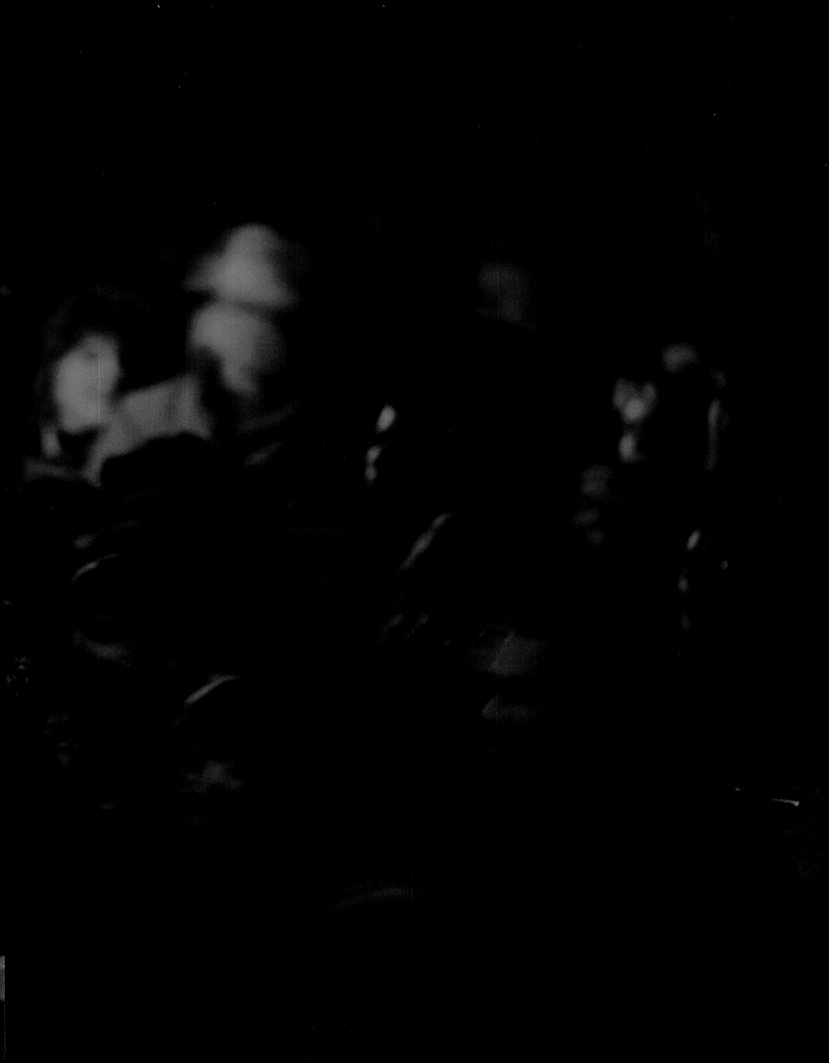

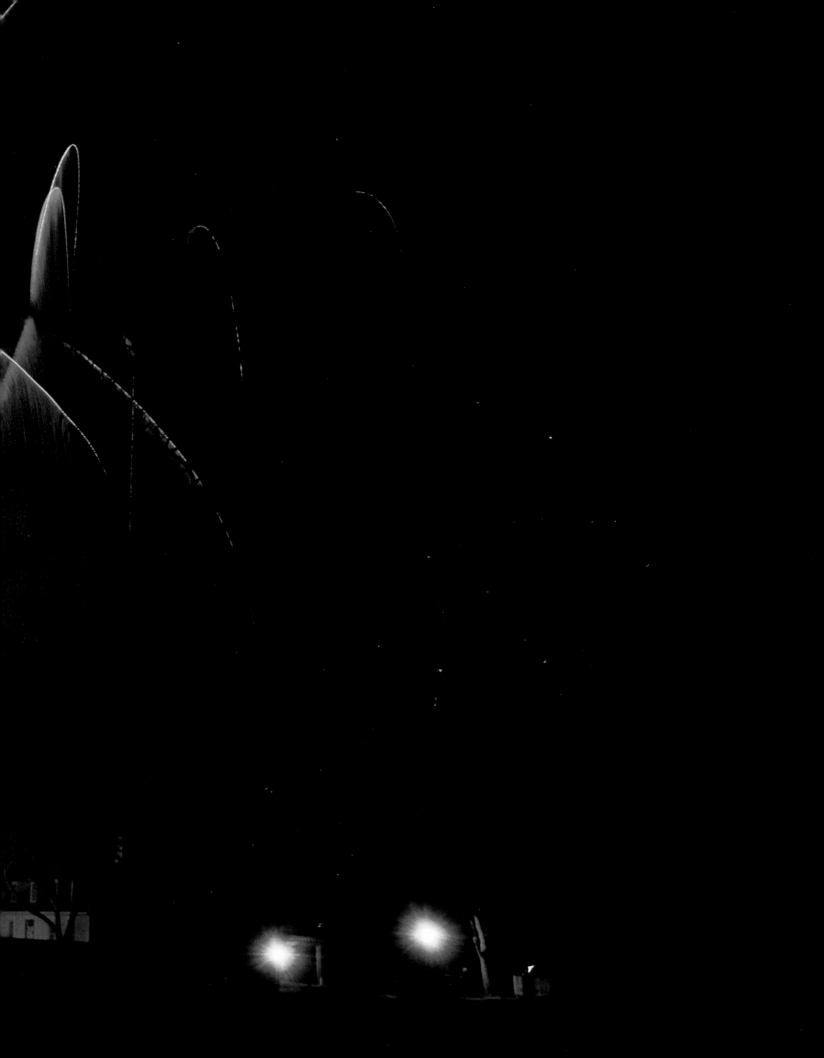

Homecoming Parade

*Football, frivolity, food and fashion mingle, as they have for generations here.
Old school club ties. Button-down, oxford-cloth shirts. Madras green trousers.
Navy blazers. Baggy Bermuda shorts. Fraternity jerseys. Sorority pins.
Discreet flasks made of hammered silver and filled with good bourbon. Coolers
of iced beer and wicker baskets of fried chicken stashed in cars behind the
stadium. Reunions. Gossip. Blind dates. Rush parties.*

Bob Dart, Cox News Service, from "The Way Football Was Meant
To Be", November, 1986

Homecoming Weekend

William and Mary Hall

What began in Lexington and ended at Yorktown derived much of its meaning and vitality from the campuses of Cambridge and Williamsburg. In a most literal sense, The College of William and Mary has withstood the trials of fire and war, and in its own right has demonstrated that faith and perseverance are enduring qualities of greatness.

President John F. Kennedy, 1961

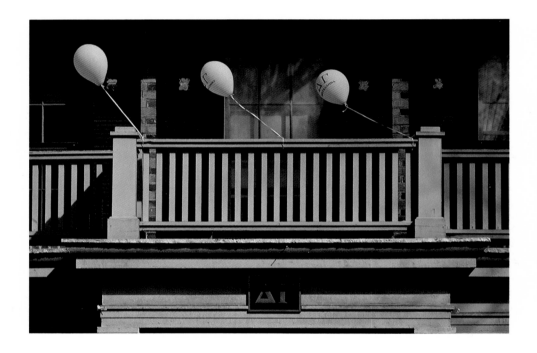

Overleaf: Homecoming Dance, Trinkle Hall

Barrett Hall

So I would extend my heartiest good wishes to The College of William and Mary, built early in the morning of American life, dedicated to the education of the makers of a great Republic, seeking to enrich and broaden the meaning of education and seeking, above all things, to recognize that Republican institutions are, in the last analysis, the application to human affairs of those broad humane ideals that a liberal education preserves, enriches and expands in our beloved land.

President Franklin D. Roosevelt, 1934

There will be times when you will feel a compulsion to return here, to walk the streets of Williamsburg, to find new meaning in the reenactments of historic scenes, to stroll this campus and give silent thanks for what it represents. When you do return, you will find, as many men great and small have found before you, that fundamental values do not change, that integrity, honesty, responsibility, a consideration for the rights of others, a belief in the dignity of the individual and the certainty of Divine guidance, will steady you in times of stress and remain a lantern to guide you as you walk along new paths.

Gov. Albertis S. Harrison, Jr., 1963

...*from these portals graduates will go forth into every nook and cranny of this great nation, bearing the indelible mark of William and Mary on their minds, their characters, their very souls...and when they long for the snows of yester-year, they will look back with pride, pleasure and satisfaction, resting secure in the knowledge that whatever else befalls, down through the ages, this Old College will endure.*

Dr. Edward E. Brickell, 1979

Reverend James Blair, William and Mary's first president 1693 - 1743

A LOOK BACK AT THE COLLEGE
OF WILLIAM AND MARY IN PICTURES

The William and Mary faculty bought the statue of Lord Botetourt at the turn of the 19th century. Many graduates of the College will remember this statue standing in front of the Wren Building until 1958.

The College building is portrayed in this painting, ca. 1820.

A student group in front of the Wren Building in 1875.

(Left to right) L.B. Wharton, President Benjamin Stoddert Ewell, Thomas T.L. Snead, George T. Wilmer, Richard A. Wise, and Charles S. Dodd comprised the William and Mary faculty in 1873.

In 1888, the College library was located in the rear of the chapel of the Wren Building.

President Ewell with Professor Hugh Bird, the youngest professor at the College in 1888.

The "Seven Wise Men" in 1888: Hugh S. Bird, Thomas Jefferson Stubbs, Charles E. Bishop, and (seated) Rev. Lyman B. Wharton, President Lyon G. Tyler, Van Franklin Garrett and John Leslie Hall.

(Left) The staff of the *William and Mary College Monthly* in 1899. The *Monthly* was the College's first student publication.

(Below) An Alumni Banquet in 1897.

At the turn of the century, the Brafferton was used as a dormitory. That's Jamestown Road in the foreground.

Women were admitted to William and Mary for the first time in 1918. This is the freshman class picture from that year.

I was born and raised within the shadows of this old college, scarcely a stone's throw from this room. I played and worked daily upon this campus. I sat at the feet of that small group of saints and scholars who awoke this College from her sleep and passed her on to her present glory and more glorious future.

No one not made of marble could have lived and grown so close and so long to this old College in that day without developing a sentiment, which time and separation cannot erase.

Joseph F. Hall, June 11, 1938

World War I is reflected in the uniforms of these men in Tyler Hall, 1918.

President Warren G. Harding receives an honorary doctor of laws degree in 1921, at the inauguration of Dr. J.A.C. Chandler as president of the College.

President Calvin Coolidge addressed a Virginia sesquicentennial crowd at the Wren Building, May, 1926.

Football coaches Carl Voyles (right) and Ruben McCray coached back-to-back from 1939 through 1950, compiling some of the best records in Tribe history.

The boat house at Lake Matoaka was built in 1935. Four years later, these students enjoyed some canoeing on the lake.

President Harry S. Truman received an honorary doctor of laws degree in 1948.

The dining room at Trinkle Hall in the early 1950s, before it became "The Pub."

October 16, 1957 — Queen Elizabeth and Prince Phillip visit Williamsburg and the College in connection with the 350th anniversary of the English settlement of Virginia. She spoke to a large crowd from the balcony of the Wren Building.

For years "Ducs" curtsied and bowed to Lord Botetourt as part of orientation week. This shot is from 1953.

(Left) The cozy confines of Blow Gym, when the noise was deafening. Tribe teams rarely lost at home, especially in the year shown above, 1960. That's Ben Vaughn shooting a layup against Virginia Tech.

(Below) HRH Prince Charles becomes a lifetime fellow at the College, May 4, 1981. The convocation was held at Phi Beta Kappa Hall.